DAREDEVILS' GUIDES

A DAREDEVIL'S
GUIDE TO
CAR RACING

by Robb Murray

Leslie Mark Kendall, Curator
Petersen Automotive Museum
Los Angeles, California

CAPSTONE PRESS
a capstone imprint

Velocity Books are published by Capstone Press,
1710 Roe Crest Drive, North Mankato, Minnesota 56003
www.capstonepub.com

Library of Congress Cataloging-in-Publication Data
Murray., Robb.
A daredevil's guide to car racing / by Robb Murray.
p. cm. — (Daredevils' guides.)
Includes bibliographical references and index.
ISBN 978-1-4296-9986-0 (library binding)
ISBN 978-1-4765-1803-9 (ebook pdf)
1. Automobile racing—Juvenile literature. I. Title.
GV1029.13.M87 2013
796.72—dc23   2012034344

Editorial Credits
Mandy Robbins, editor; Veronica Scott, designer; Laura Manthe, production specialist

Photo Credits
AP Images: Corbis/Bettmann, 19 (inset), David Maung, 32, Mike Conroy, 21 (inset),
Ric Feld, 27; Corbis: Bettmann, 7 (top); Dreamstime: Ashley Dickerson, cover (bottom),
Gorgios, 14; Newscom: Getty Images/AFP/Jean-Francois Monier, 22-23, Icon SMI 796/
Doug Murray, 39 (middle), Icon SMI/Bill Shipley, 36, Image Broker/uwe kraft, 41, MCT/
David T. Foster III, 29, Photoshot/Icon SMI/Matt Bolt, 30-31, UPI/Martin Fried, 45, ZUMA
Press/Action Press/XPB, 20-21, ZUMA Press/Cityfiles, 37, ZUMA Press/Ron Bijlsma, 15;
Shutterstock: Action Sports Photography, 4-5, 12-13, 18-19, 24, 43 (both), ANATOMIA3D, 25,
Beelde Photography, 8, CHEN WS, 34, Christopher Halloran, 35, Darren Brode, 6 (bottom),
de2marco, 11, Doug James, 6 (top), EPG_EuroPhotoGraphics, 39 (bottom), 42, Hodag Media,
9, john j. klaiber jr., 10, 17 (top), Kirill_M, 17 (bottom), Natursports, cover (top left), 1 (left),
Photo Works, cover (top right), 1 (right), Steve Mann, 7 (bottom), Tatiana Popova, 16,
Tomislav Forgo, 19 (money), windu, 20 (bricks); Wikimedia: Agence de presse Meurisse, 44

Artistic Effects
Shutterstock: Angela Waye, argus, bioraven, Eky Studio, gigello, Iscatel, Joseph Sevcik,
kakin, leungchopan, Leyn, LongQuattro, muschmule, Nataliia Natykach, prudkov, rodho,
Roman Sotola, Unscrew,

Printed in the United States of America in Stevens Point, Wisconsin.
092012   006937WZS13

Table
of Contents

ARE YOU DAREDEVIL ENOUGH?

You see a hot car cruising down the road on a sunny day, and something stirs inside you. You begin to imagine you're behind the wheel of that car. Or maybe you pretend you're Jeff Gordon, weaving in and out of a crowded race field at 170 miles (274 kilometers) per hour. Maybe you imagine you're Dario Franchitti, crossing the finish line at Indianapolis Motor Speedway. The crowd goes wild!

Car racing is a daredevil's game. It's fast and dangerous. Only the bravest and most skilled drivers earn the sport's highest honors. Since its earliest days in the late 1800s, car racing has come a long way. Today it is one of the world's great spectator sports.

Car racing may seem simple—just put the pedal to the metal. But it takes physical conditioning, precision, and quick thinking. It also requires a willingness to step into a world full of danger.

Chapter 1

BUILT FOR SPEED

Car racing has been around for more than 100 years. From the very beginning, race car drivers and designers have been pushing their cars to faster speeds.

NASCAR stock car

Indy car

How Far Can Each Car Travel in an Hour?

Duryeas' Car

| 7 miles | 11 miles |

Lemaître's Car

Slow Beginnings

The car that won the very first car race on record had a simple, 3.5-**horsepower** engine. The race took place in France in 1894 and was officially called a "reliability test." The goal was to see which car model was the most reliable. The course went from the city of Paris to Rouen. Albert Lemaître was the official winner. He completed the 78-mile (126-km) race in just under seven hours.

The first race on American soil was actually slower than the Paris race, but its drivers faced snowy weather conditions. The race took place in 1895. The winners, brothers Charles and Frank Duryea, covered 54 miles (87 km) in 10 hours.

Duryea brothers' car

Fast-forward 120 years. The difference in engine power is like comparing a snail to a cheetah. Drivers in the National Association for Stock Car Auto Racing (NASCAR) circuit reach up to 180 miles (290 km) per hour. Indy cars can reach 250 miles (402 km) per hour. And the fastest drag racers reach 330 miles (531 km) per hour!

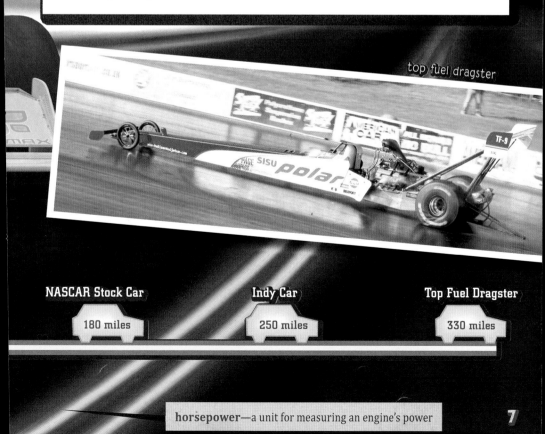

top fuel dragster

NASCAR Stock Car
180 miles

Indy Car
250 miles

Top Fuel Dragster
330 miles

horsepower—a unit for measuring an engine's power

Comparing Cars

Engines aren't the only car parts that have been improved. The bodies of race cars have changed a lot. In the early days of auto racing, little thought was put into **aerodynamic** designs. Today race car designers keep **downforce** in mind. Downforce keeps a car from flying off the track at high speeds. More downforce means cars have a better grip on the track and can take corners at higher speeds. But vehicles look different from each other depending on what type of racing they are built for. Different types of racing require different body features.

NASCAR Stock Cars

Engines start out at about 300 horsepower but are then modified to increase speed. Exhaust systems, which decrease horsepower, are removed.

Splitters help the car hug the road at high speeds. They do this by keeping low air pressure beneath the car and high air pressure above it.

Tires on NASCAR vehicles are smooth so that all of the tires' rubber is in contact with the track. The more rubber touching the road, the more traction a car has.

Indy Cars

Indy cars run on V6 engines that can get up to 700 horsepower.

Front and rear wings create downforce to help the driver control the vehicle.

Tires on Indy cars are wide to increase traction. In dry weather, Indy cars use tires with no tread. But if the weather gets wet, they can be replaced with treaded tires. The treads push water away from the tires to keep cars from skidding across wet tracks.

Fact:

Indy cars create a lot of downforce. At 140 miles (225 km) per hour, they could drive upside down in a tunnel.

A spoiler runs along the top of the car's tail end. Spoilers work like the wings of a plane, but in reverse. Airplane wings are designed to lift the plane off the ground. A spoiler's job is to push the car down, helping it hug the track.

aerodynamic—designed to reduce air resistance
downforce—the force of passing air pressing down on a moving vehicle
modify—to change in some way
traction—the grip of a car's tires on the ground

9

Sprint cars have a large winglike panel mounted on their roofs. These panels are designed to provide downforce and help the cars manage tough corners.

Like stock cars, rally cars can have spoilers to produce more downforce.

Sprint Cars

Sprint cars race on small, oval dirt tracks. A sprint car's powerful V8 engine can produce up to 810 horsepower.

Tires on sprint cars have low air pressure. Having less air in the tires improves traction when cornering on dirt tracks. Big, sharp tread patterns on the tires help the cars grip dirt. The back tires on sprint cars are staggered. The right tire is bigger than the left. This setup makes the constant left turns easier to navigate.

Rally Cars

Pro rally car engines are similar to engines in everyday cars, but with a little more power. The engines have larger pistons and valves and are built with stronger parts than regular car engines. A turbocharger shoots compressed air into the engine, giving it a boost of horsepower.

Chapter 2

RACING FOR EVERY KIND OF DAREDEVIL

There are many kinds of auto racing. Different organizations manage and schedule races for different types of vehicles. Check out a few of the most popular types of car racing.

Stock Car Racing

NASCAR organizes stock car races in the United States. More than 200 pro drivers compete in races annually. In the early days of stock car racing, the cars were just that—stock cars. These cars were part of an automaker's regular lineup of cars available for purchase. Over the years, NASCAR changed the rules about what drivers could do to their cars. Today the cars circling the tracks are hardly the kind of machines sold at local dealerships.

Gladiator Endurance

NASCAR is the most popular stock car racing series in the United States, but there are others. In the Gladiator Endurance Auto Racing series only true stock cars are allowed. No significant changes can be made to the engine, body, or suspension system. Events are similar in nature to those of NASCAR. Races consist of up to 250 laps and are held at tracks in Wisconsin and Illinois.

Fact:

NASCAR races consist of a various number of laps with points given to drivers depending on how well they finish. At the end of the season, the driver with the most points wins the championship.

Drag Racing

Drag racing began in the 1940s when people fixed up **hot rods** to race in the California deserts. Two cars would sit side-by-side and then take off along a straight path. In seconds the winner was celebrating victory. The format of drag racing hasn't changed much since then.

Wally Parks started the National Hot Rod Association (NHRA) in 1951 to organize drag racing and make it safer. Today the NHRA hosts drag racing events all over the nation. The most well-known drag racing cars are top fuel dragsters, pro stock cars, and funny cars.

Unlike other types of racing, drag racers race in a straight line. Most dragsters race on tracks that are 0.25 mile (0.4 km) long. Top fuel and funny car drag racers face off on tracks that are 320 feet (98 meters) shorter.

Fact:

Street racing began in the early 1900s, and it's exactly what it sounds like. Drivers race each other on public roads. Street racing is illegal, and it can be deadly.

Indy Car Racing

Indy car racing has **open-wheel race cars** that race in various circuits, most notably the IZOD IndyCar Series. Races are held throughout North America. Most races are on large oval tracks. Other races are on street courses through cities. Indy car racing is named after the IZOD circuit's biggest race of the year—the Indianapolis 500.

hot rod—a car or pickup improved for better performance
open-wheel race car—a race car with the wheels outside the car's main body

Sprint Car Racing

Sprint car races take place on dirt tracks. The cars, especially those in the winged-car division, have a unique look. The premier sprint car racing circuit is called World of Outlaws. Many drivers raced sprint cars before finding fame in other types of racing. These drivers include Jeff Gordon, Mario Andretti, A.J. Foyt, and Al Unser Jr.

Rally Racing

Rally car racing, unlike most other types of racing, doesn't take place on a track. Instead, racers compete on closed courses that span rugged terrain or city streets. Often pairs or teams of drivers race together. The most popular rally racing circuit is World Rally Championship (WRC). Rally racing is among the most dangerous forms of auto racing. Some races, such as the Dakar Rally, have seen many drivers and fans die in crashes.

Formula One

Formula One (F1) racing is based in Europe. F1 cars are open-wheel cars that look similar to Indy cars. F1 cars race on courses that have twists and turns. Sometimes they also race on closed public roads. Cars reach speeds of up to 210 miles (338 km) per hour. Like many other kinds of racing, Formula One works on a points system.

Chapter 3

OFF TO THE RACES

In all racing circuits there are races that stand out. Drivers train hard all year long looking forward to these exciting events.

Daytona 500

For NASCAR drivers and fans, the Daytona 500 is the race of all races. It is the first race of the season and is typically held in late February. The race consists of 200 laps around the 2.5-mile (4-km) Daytona International Speedway in Daytona Beach, Florida. The first Daytona 500 took place in 1959. Fifty-nine racers faced off in front of 41,000 fans. The winner was Lee Petty.

Dale Earnhardt Sr. holds the record for most times completing all 500 miles (805 km) of the race. He did this 14 times. It took him 20 tries, however, before he finally won a Daytona 500. Tragically, Earnhardt died on the final lap of the 2001 Daytona 500.

When a driver wins the Daytona 500, he takes home more than $1 million in prize money. In 2012 Daytona 500 winner Matt Kenseth won $1,589,387.

Fact:

The 2007 Daytona 500 had a very close finish. Kevin Harvick beat Mark Martin by just .02 seconds. It was the narrowest win margin in Daytona history.

The supreme king of the Daytona 500 is Lee Petty's son, Richard Petty. With seven Daytona 500 wins, he boasts the most Daytona victories of any racer.

Indianapolis 500

If you think bigger is better, you need to check out the Indianapolis Motor Speedway in Indiana. It's the world's largest spectator sport facility. The Churchill Downs horse racing track, Yankee Stadium, the Rose Bowl, and Vatican City could all fit inside the track's 253 acres (102 hectares). It has about 250,000 permanent seats but draws as many as 400,000 spectators.

One of the track's nicknames is "the brickyard." This comes from the 3.2 million paving bricks that line the bottom of the speedway. Most of it is now covered with asphalt. A thin strip remains visible, however. One of the track's traditions is for Indy 500 winners to kiss the bricks.

Three men are tied for the most Indy 500 wins. A.J. Foyt, Al Unser Sr., and Rick Mears have each reached the winner's circle four times. Arie Luyendyk holds the record for fastest average speed at nearly 186 miles (299 km) per hour.

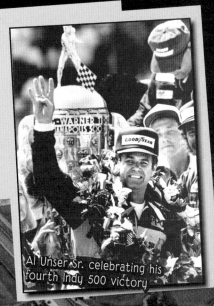

Al Unser Sr. celebrating his fourth Indy 500 victory

Fact:

Three holes of the Brickyard Crossing Golf Course are inside the track's oval. They are accessible by an underground tunnel.

24 Hours of Le Mans

The 24 Hours of Le Mans was first held in 1923. It is one of the oldest races in the world. It's also one of the toughest. The object is simple: be the team that can cover the most distance on the closed track in 24 hours.

The race is a challenge for several reasons. The driving alone is demanding. Each driving team must have at least three drivers. Drivers race at high speeds and navigate tight corners for up to two hours at a time. To win the race, teams must be smart about speed and fuel. Faster speeds burn more fuel, which means more pit stops. More pit stops reduce time spent driving. Running at high speeds for many hours in the middle of summer takes a toll on the cars too. Durability and quick repairs are key.

Fact:

The deadliest crash in racing history occurred during the 24 Hours of Le Mans race. In 1955 Pierre Levegh's car veered off the track and into the stands. The crash killed Levegh and at least 84 fans.

Chapter 4

IN THE DRIVER'S SEAT

Driving a high-performance vehicle requires more than just the ability to step on the gas. Increased heart rates and the pressure put on bodies at extreme speeds require drivers to be fit.

Carl Edwards

Carl Edwards is one of NASCAR's fittest athletes. In 2011 Edwards was brought into ESPN's Sport Science lab to judge his reaction time under extreme conditions. Edwards did well in a series of difficult visual tests. The researchers cranked up the sound during the tests to mimic noise levels inside a race car. Then they put him through a stationary bike workout and had him retest his reaction times. Edwards' time actually improved!

Many drivers do weight training that mimics driving. Some training machines are set up to isolate arm, chest, and neck muscles while simulating driving a race car. Many drivers also train by swimming or running in an effort to build up their stamina.

In 2005 researchers at the University of Jyvaskyla in Finland studied the effects of race car driving on drivers' bodies. Researchers found that race car driving actually wore down a person's muscles more than the difficult sport of rowing. The study was also able to pinpoint which types of drivers were the strongest. It was found that Indy car racers have stronger necks, hand grips, shoulders, and legs. Rally drivers had stronger feet and abdomens.

Fact:

Drivers need stamina to face the hot temperatures inside a race car. In closed cockpit cars, a driver may sweat off up to 6.6 pounds (3 kilograms) during a race. This can lead to dehydration.

dehydration—a life-threatening medical condition caused by a lack of water

Going Head-To-Head

In car racing, there are millions of dollars and untold glory at stake. It's no wonder the heated competition has resulted in some pretty intense conflicts. Here are some of the most tense driver encounters in car racing.

1979
DONNIE ALLISON vs. CALE YARBOROUGH

This feud blew up during the final lap of the 1979 Daytona 500. It also happened to be the first entire NASCAR race to be televised. Cale Yarborough was coming up behind Donnie Allison and bumped him as he tried to pass on the inside. The bump resulted in both cars spinning into the infield. The two drivers immediately got out of the cars and started to argue about who caused the wreck. It wasn't long before punches were thrown. The brawl left a lasting first impression on TV viewers and brought more fans to the sport.

1997
ARIE LUYENDYK
vs.
A.J. FOYT

This feud began in the winner's circle after a 1997 Indy car race in Fort Worth, Texas. A.J. Foyt's team was celebrating their win when Arie Luyendyk showed up insisting he'd won the race. The argument got physical, and Foyt eventually shoved Luyendyk to the ground. It was all caught on tape, and Foyt later apologized. He was fined $20,000, and Luyendyk was fined $14,000. Luyendyk was eventually named as the race winner. But Foyt refused to give the original trophy back!

Donnie Allison and Gale Yarborough at the 1979 Daytona 500

2008

KEVIN HARVICK vs. CARL EDWARDS

This feud began with some name calling. Carl Edwards had bumped Kevin Harvick and knocked him out of a 2008 NASCAR race. Angry, Harvick called Edwards a "pansy" during a nationally televised interview. Harvick and Edwards met again at Lowe's Motor Speedway in North Carolina. This time, name calling turned to pushing and shoving. Bad blood remained until 2011, when the pair decided to put their differences aside. Edwards even made a $15,000 donation to a charity Harvick runs to help orphans.

2011

KYLE BUSCH vs. RICHARD CHILDRESS

Sometimes NASCAR fights involve people who aren't even drivers! Kyle Busch rubbed racing team owner Richard Childress the wrong way. On the cool-down lap of a race, Busch's car made contact with a car driven by one of Childress' drivers. Afterward, Childress tracked Busch down, put him in a headlock, and punched him several times. NASCAR fined Childress $150,000 and put him on probation for one year.

2012
ERICA ENDERS
vs.
GREG ANDERSON

Pro stock drag racer Erica Enders earned her first professional win on July 1, 2012. She beat four-time champion Greg Anderson in the first-ever Pro Stock class win by a woman. Anderson had commented earlier that he didn't want to be "that guy" who lost to Enders when she finally won. To celebrate her win, Enders was photographed with her trophy in front of Anderson's trailer. He later blasted her behavior as unprofessional.

Enders and Anderson joking around at a race prior to Enders' win

probation—a period of time for testing a person's behavior or job qualifications; it may be used as a punishment for bad behavior

29

Chapter 5

DANGER AT THE RACES

When you pair monstrous engines with competitive drivers, destruction is bound to occur from time to time. In many cases, crashes are a result of aggressive driving. When cars bump each other, they often lose traction and spin out. They may crash into the wall or each other, or they end up in the middle of the track.

Crashes are quite common. Between 2001 and 2006 there were 1,320 crashes in NASCAR alone. Fans aren't immune to danger either. Over the years, several tragedies have occurred that have claimed the lives of fans.

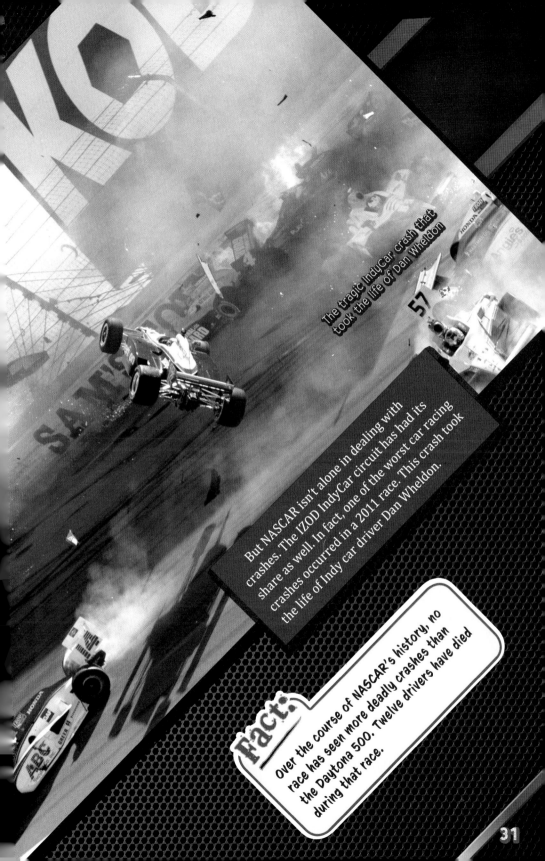

The tragic IndyCar crash that took the life of Dan Wheldon

But NASCAR isn't alone in dealing with crashes. The IZOD IndyCar circuit has had its share as well. In fact, one of the worst car racing crashes occurred in a 2011 race. This crash took the life of Indy car driver Dan Wheldon.

Fact:

Over the course of NASCAR's history, no race has seen more deadly crashes than the Daytona 500. Twelve drivers have died during that race.

DANGEROUS RACES AROUND THE WORLD

While the crashes in NASCAR and IndyCar races may get most of the attention, they're not the most dangerous racing venues. A handful of races around the world are much more dangerous.

Baja 1000

One of the best-known races for thrill seekers is the Baja 1000. It is part of the SCORE Championship Desert Racing series. This race rumbles across 1,000 miles (1,609 km) of Mexico's rough and rocky terrain. A new off-road course is designed every year. Spectators often add obstacles to the course that the drivers don't know about. In the past they've dug holes and built ramps on the course. At least 25 drivers have been killed during this race.

Fans cheer on a racer during the 2004 Baja 1000.

Dakar Rally

The Dakar Rally is known as the most dangerous sporting event in the world. Since 1978, 49 people have been killed in the race. It is held on rugged terrain, such as deserts and jungles. Motorcycles, cars, and trucks race in the Dakar Rally. Competitors are given a map of the course and must find their own way. The race originally began in Paris and traveled across Europe and the deserts of Africa before ending in Dakar, Senegal. The 2012 route went through Argentina, Peru, and Chile. The course was 8,000 miles (12,875 km) long and took about two weeks to finish.

Macau Grand Prix

The Macau Grand Prix in China is another dangerous race. It takes place on inner-city streets that have been blocked off from civilian drivers. Drivers must navigate around tight corners at high speeds. Injuries and deaths are not uncommon.

Arsenio Laurel was the first person to die in the Macau Grand Prix. He had won the race in 1962 and 1963. But Laurel died in the 1967 Macau Grand Prix when his car skidded out of control and crashed into a wall.

In the Pits

Most of the danger in car racing is faced by the drivers. But pit crews are also at risk. These daring individuals change the tires and fill gas tanks at lightning fast speeds.

Jackman Gets Squeezed

T.J. Ford was a jackman on NASCAR driver Paul Menard's crew. It was Ford's job to raise the car's front and back for tire changes. During a race in 2007, Ford was about to lift the rear of Menard's car for a tire change. Just then, driver David Stremme drove his car into Ford. Luckily, Ford escaped with only a knee injury.

IndyCar Pit Collision

Bad brakes wreaked havoc in the pits at an IZOD IndyCar race in Toronto in July 2012. Driver Justin Wilson's brakes failed as he was about to drive into pit row. His car pinned pit crew worker Chuck Homan between two cars, giving him a serious leg injury. Another pit crew member suffered an ankle injury. Two others were treated at the scene for minor injuries.

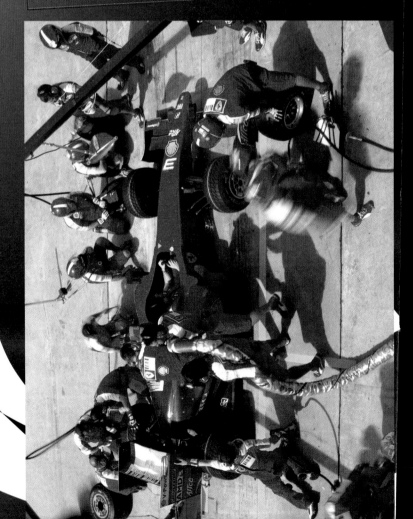

Tire To the Head

Art Harris was a gas man for NASCAR driver Michael Waltrip's car in 2007. It was his job to fill the fuel cell with gas. But during one pit stop, Harris got bopped in the head by a loose tire from another driver's car. He was taken out of the pit on a stretcher and sent to the hospital in an ambulance.

Tragedy in the Pits

The worst pit row accident in NASCAR racing history occurred in 1990 and turned out to be fatal. Ricky Rudd was driving into pit row when he lost control of his car. The car struck Mike Rich, Bill Elliott's rear tire changer. Rich died from his injuries.

The Fallen

Race car drivers defy death with each turn. Unfortunately, some have sacrificed their lives competing in the sport they love.

Ayrton Senna

F1 driver Ayrton Senna died in a crash in 1994 at the San Marino Grand Prix. He was leading the race at the time. Before his death, Senna had won three F1 world championships.

Dale Earnhardt Sr.

Dale Earnhardt Sr. was one of NASCAR's most beloved drivers. He died on the final lap of the Daytona 500 in 2001. Earnhardt was an aggressive driver with a big personality. His death prompted an outpouring of emotion from fans. His trademark Number 3 is still seen on cars and jackets today.

Dan Wheldon

In 2011 a fatal crash took the life of young Indy car driver Dan Wheldon. Wheldon won the 2011 Indianapolis 500, marking the second time the British driver had won the race. It was the biggest moment of his career. Months later, he died in a crash at the Las Vegas Indy 300.

Gareth Roberts

In 2012 a crash in Sicily, Italy, claimed the life of rally car co-driver Gareth Roberts. Roberts was navigating for Irish driver Craig Breen in the Targa Florio rally when their car crashed. Their car struck a guard rail, killing Roberts instantly and injuring Breen.

Chapter 6

IMPROVING RACING SAFETY

In car racing, dangerous crashes often lead to safety improvements. Many of these changes directly affect the vehicles drivers race.

Fuel Cells

Fuel cells came into use in the 1960s after stock car driver Glenn Roberts crashed in 1964. During the crash, gas leaked from Roberts' car. The gas fueled a fire that left Roberts with severe burns, which later killed him. Since then, racing teams on all major circuits have used rubber cells inside the gas tank. These fuel cells limit fuel leakage in case of a crash.

Roll Cages

Some version of a roll cage has been around since the 1950s. No matter what kind of race car a driver has, the science behind the roll cage is the same. It keeps the weight of the car off the driver if the car flips. This safety feature began as a roll bar. Today it's a full roll cage to give the driver protection on all sides.

Restrictor Plates

Restrictor plates are used in NASCAR races to limit how fast cars can go. The plates are made of metal and have holes drilled into them. Restrictor plates limit the amount of air flowing into the car's engine. Limiting airflow makes the car go slower.

Head and Neck Support (HANS) Devices

Race officials believe a HANS device could have saved Dale Earnhardt Sr.'s life. A HANS device is a collar that attaches a driver's helmet to the seat behind him or her. It prevents violent head-snapping during a crash.

On the Track

In 2000 Indy car managers decided to improve the tracks to prevent injuries. They worked with engineers from the University of Nebraska to create Steel And Foam Energy Reduction (SAFER) barriers. The barriers absorb impacts, making crashing into them less violent. In 2002 the Indianapolis Motor Speedway became the first track to install the barriers. Since then they have also been installed at other Indy car tracks as well as NASCAR tracks.

The Last Line of Defense

A driver's last line of defense is the protective clothing and gear he or she wears. Many racing crashes involve open flames. Nearly every piece of equipment a driver wears is designed to provide fire protection. Skin can burn at 140 degrees Fahrenheit (60 degrees Celsius). A gasoline fire can burn up to 1,650°F (899°C).

Jumpsuits

Jumpsuits cover nearly all of a racer's body. They must allow free movement, while also being **fire retardant**. A high-quality suit made of the fire retardant material Nomex can cost $1,500.

Gloves

Racing gloves vary widely in price. Like jumpsuits, the best gloves are made of Nomex. They cost more than $200. But top-quality gloves can mean the difference between hands a driver can use, or hands undergoing skin-replacement surgeries.

Shoes

A driver's shoes must be flexible enough for the driver to hit the gas or brake quickly. They must also be able to resist flames in the event of a crash. Good fire retardant racing shoes cost about $300.

fire retardant—able to resist fire

Helmets

At the speeds that drivers race, helmets are a must. In a crash, a helmet can prevent a brain injury and save a driver's life. Helmets cost up to $5,000.

Chapter 7

TOP GUNS

Every sport has its legends, and car racing is no different. With talent and dedication, these drivers never gave up on their goal to make it to the top.

MARIO ANDRETTI

Mario Andretti is one of the greatest drivers in the history of car racing. He was named Indy Racing League's Rookie of the Year in 1965. Andretti began with Indy cars, then moved to F1 racing. He also competed in NASCAR races and won the 1967 Daytona 500.

Andretti Quick Facts:

only driver to win Daytona 500, Indianapolis 500, and F1 championships

retired in 1994 after $11 million in winnings

Fact:
The Indy Racing League was a precursor to today's IZOD IndyCar series.

RICHARD PETTY

Richard Petty has more NASCAR wins than any other driver. He also has a fitting nickname—the King. Petty was the first stock car driver to make more than $1 million in earnings.

Petty Quick Facts:

- began racing in 1958
- won the Daytona 500 seven times
- won the NASCAR national championship seven times
- won 200 NASCAR races

DON GARLITS

Don "Big Daddy" Garlits is a drag racing legend. During his 40 years of drag racing, he earned 144 national event titles.

Garlits Quick Facts:

- began racing in 1950
- won the NHRA U.S. Nationals a record eight times
- won 17 NHRA Championships

43

WOMEN IN RACING

Throughout its history, car racing has been dominated by men, but women have always been on the racing scene. In recent years, their ranks have grown.

Hellé Nice

Frenchwoman Hellé Nice broke into car racing in 1929. Early in her career, she sped to victory in an all-female race called the Grand Prix Feminin. Her skills and success earned her the nickname "The Queen of Speed."

Shirley Muldowney

Shirley Muldowney was a drag racing pioneer. She started racing in the 1960s and became one of the top racers of her day. In 1971 Muldowney made the switch from top fuel dragsters to funny cars. That same year, she won her very first funny car race. Muldowney's long and successful career spanned 40 years.

Johanna Long

Johanna Long may be the next big name among female racers. As a youth, she raced in a number of different lower-level racing series. At the age of 19, she entered the world of professional NASCAR racing in 2010.

Car racing continues to grow and evolve. The rise of women in racing is just one way the sport is changing. Car and safety gear technology also continues to improve and change. But one thing that will never change is the adventurous spirit that draws daredevil racers and fans to the sport.

Glossary

aerodynamic (ayr-oh-dy-NA-mik)—designed to reduce air resistance

dehydration (dee-hy-DRAY-shuhn)—a life-threatening medical condition caused by a lack of water

downforce (DOUN-fors)—the force of passing air pressing down on a moving vehicle

exhaust (ig-ZAWST)—the waste gasses produced by an engine

fire retardant (FIRE ri-TAR-duhnt)—able to resist burning

horsepower (HORSS-pou-ur)—a unit for measuring an engine's power

hot rod (HOT ROD)—a car or pickup improved for better performance

modify (MOD-uh-fye)—to change in some way

open-wheel race car (OH-pen-weel RAYSS CARS)—a race car with the wheels outside the car's main body

probation (pro-BAY-shuhn)—a period of time for testing a person's behavior or job qualifications

roll cage (ROHL KAYJ)—a structure of strong metal tubing in a car that surrounds and protects drivers

series (SIHR-eez)—a schedule of races that leads to a single championship

stock car (STOK CAR)—a car built for racing on paved tracks that is based on the regular model sold to the public

traction (TRAK-shuhn)—the grip of a car's tires on the ground

Read More

Gigliotti, Jim. *Off-Road Racing*. Racing Mania. New York: Marshall Cavendish Benchmark, 2010.

McCollum, Sean. *Racecars: the Ins and Outs of Stock Cars, Dragsters, and Open-Wheelers*. RPM. Mankato, Minn.: Capstone Press, 2010.

Sheen, Barbara. *Janet Guthrie: Indy Car Racing Pionee*r. Innovators. Detroit: Kidhaven Press, 2010.

Internet Sites

FactHound offers a safe, fun way to find Internet sites related to this book. All of the sites on FactHound have been researched by our staff.

Here's all you do:

Visit *www.facthound.com*

Type in this code: 9781429699860

Index